LET'S FIND OUT ABOUT
EASTER

LET'S FIND OUT ABOUT
EASTER

by FRANKLIN WATTS

Pictures by Marta Cone

Franklin Watts, Inc.
575 Lexington Avenue
New York, New York 10022

The author's royalties are donated to the
Frederic G. Melcher Scholarship Fund

SBN 531-00018-4
Copyright © 1969 by Franklin Watts, Inc.
Library of Congress Catalog Card Number: 69-12595
Printed in the United States of America
by the Moffa Press, Inc.

3 4 5

LET'S FIND OUT ABOUT
EASTER

Easter is a spring holiday of two joys.

For the Christian it means that Christ who is the son of God has risen from the dead and promises life after death for all Christians.

For all people it is the joy of celebrating the life of a new year of nature's growth.

Flowers bloom.

Leaves come out on trees.

The grass becomes green and plants grow.

Birds lay eggs and raise their young.

Many animals are born in the spring.

    For Christians Easter comes at the end of Holy Week.

    The name Holy Week stands for the last week on earth of Jesus the Christ. He is often called Our Lord.

    Palm Sunday is the day when Jesus entered Jerusalem and people welcomed him with cheers and put palms on the streets.

17

Good Friday—the name comes from God's Friday—is the day when the Romans put Jesus on a cross to die.

In those days when a person was convicted of wrongdoing he was nailed to a cross.

Because Jesus died on the cross, Christians use a cross to represent their religion.

Many Christians go to church on Good Friday and in some states it is a Holy Day. The word holiday came from Holy Day but is now used for both Holy Days and other days of celebration.

On the first Easter Sunday, friends of Jesus went to the place where Jesus had been buried. They found that Jesus' body was not there, and were told by an angel that Jesus had risen from the dead.

For Christians Easter is the most Holy Day of the whole year.

The word Easter comes from a very old celebration that welcomed the arrival of spring.

Most people had and many still have a day to celebrate the arrival of spring and many of the customs of Easter have nothing to do with Christian teaching.

People wear new clothes to celebrate the new year of life around them.

All animal life starts with an egg so we have Easter eggs.

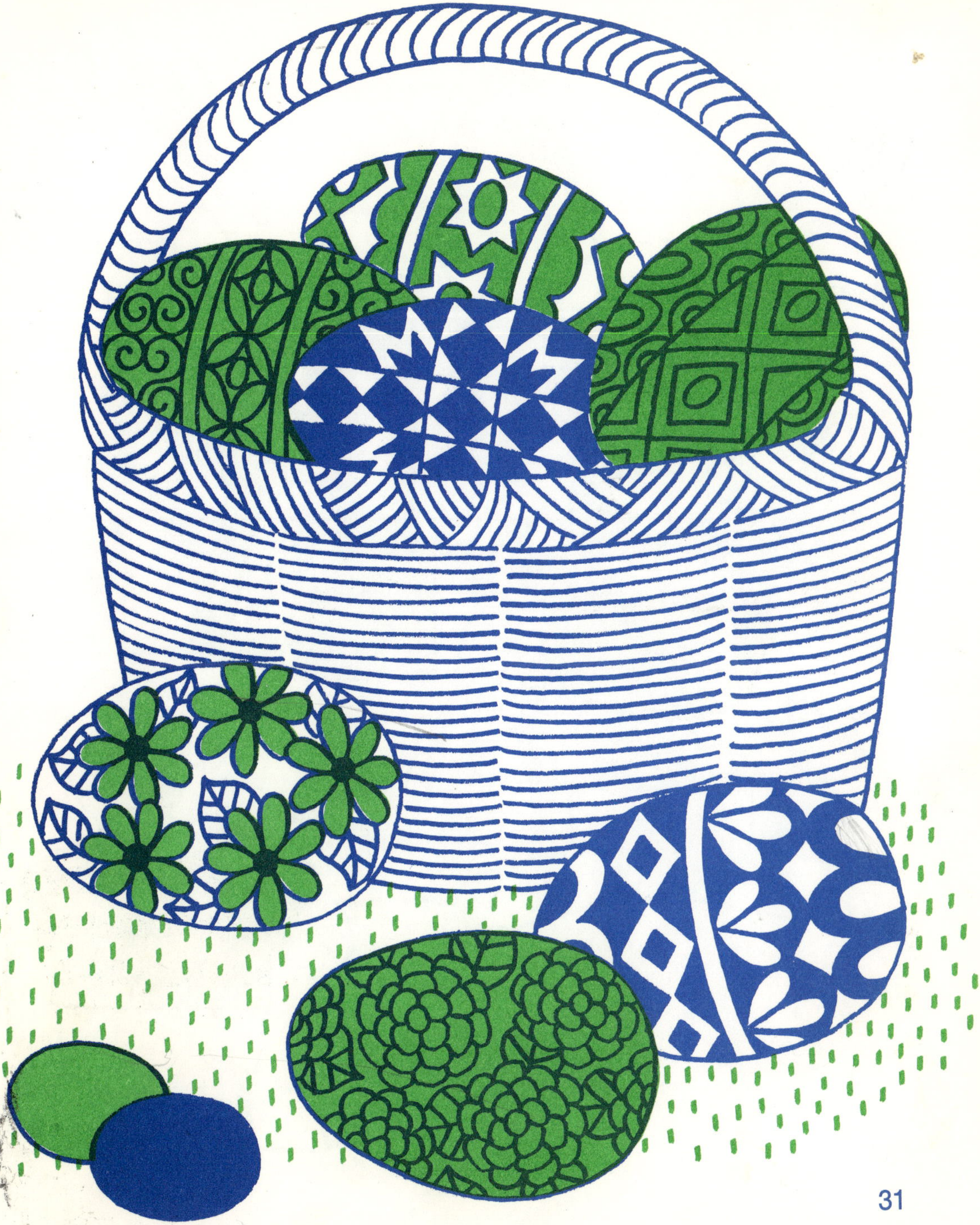

32

We have Easter rabbits because rabbits grow a lot of young very fast and represent growing life.

Without the sun there would be no life on earth. To welcome the sun on Easter day many people go to church service out-of-doors. These are called sunrise services.

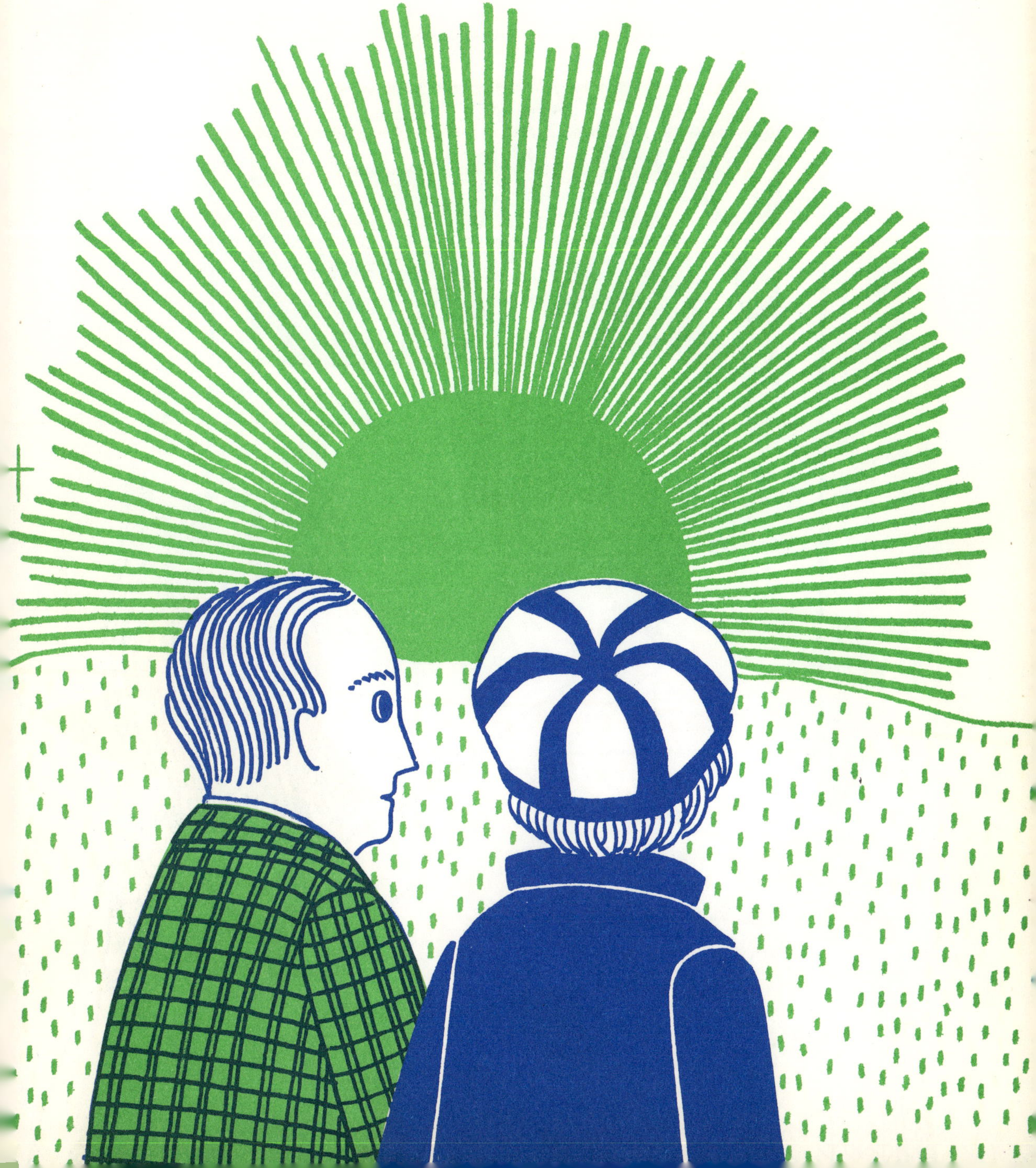

APRIL

S	M	T	W	T	F	S
	1	2	3	4	5	6
7 easter	8	9	10	11	12	
14	15	16	17	18		
21	22	23	24	25		
28	29					

Easter does not come on the same day of the year every year. It comes the first Sunday after the first full moon after the first day of spring. Thus it may fall on any day from March 22 to April 25.

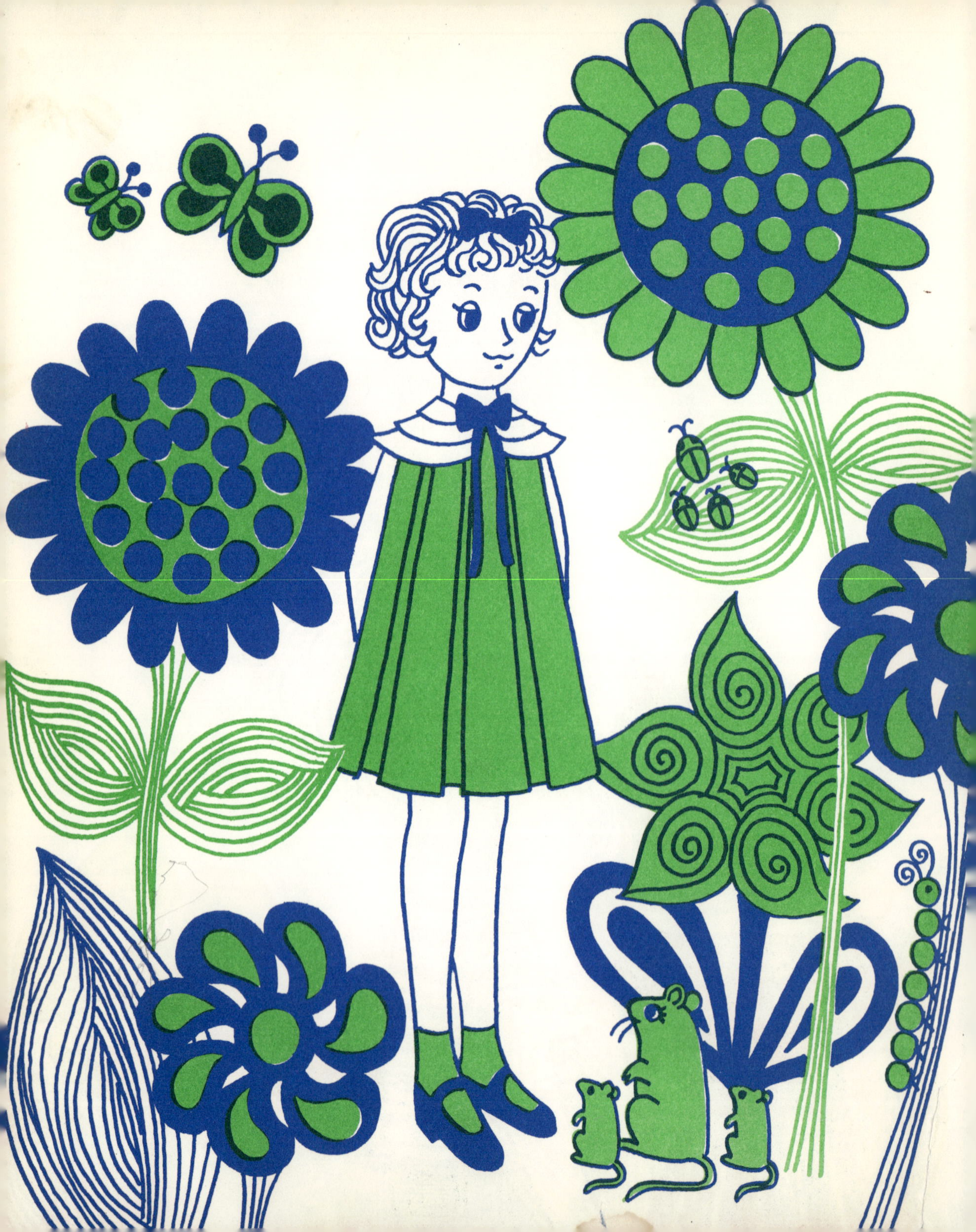

So, in thinking of Easter, remember that for Christians it is their most Holy Day. Also, it is a happy day as their Lord has risen from the dead.

For all it is a day to be glad because it represents new life about us.